Earth Day

Earth Day was first held in the United States on April 22, 1970, and was founded by United States Senator Gaylord Nelson. The second Earth Day, held on April 22, 1990, was celebrated in over 140 countries. Earth Day is a day to remind us of the need to care for our environment. It is a time to become actively involved in many Save-the-Earth projects.

Another related holiday held nationally in the United States on the last Friday of April is Arbor Day, a day to plant new trees and emphasize conservation. It was first held in Nebraska on April 10, 1872, and its founder was conservation advocate Julius Sterling Morton. The date for Arbor Day may vary depending on the state in which you live.

Activities

Start a school-wide recycling program. Collect aluminum cans, plastic bottles, paper, and glass. Put collection points around the school. If possible, have a curbside drop-off point one day a week so the public can support your efforts. Recruit some adults to help with transportation to a recycling center. This may be coordinated by your class or by your school's student government. Decide on a worthwhile organization that helps the earth and contribute the money you earn to it.

Create a bulletin board. Use the classified section of the newspaper as the background for this bulletin board. Title the board "The Daily Planet." Throughout the unit, have students bring in and post articles from newspapers or magazines that tell about environmental problems that the world is facing.

Learn how to read the air quality reports in the newspaper.

Discuss how the air can be cleaned up.

Have students design a mode of transportation that would not pollute the air.

Make a class weather station, including a wind sock, wind vane, anemometer, and rain gauge. Students can make instruments individually or in teams. Then hold an Air, Wind, and Weather Open House to share the products of the unit. Invite the school principal, parents, another class, and/or others.

Experiment to find out what makes a candle flame go out if you put a glass jar over it. Discuss how fire needs air to burn.

Cut long ribbons from tissue or crepe paper. Put music on and let students make up their own ribbon dances. Point out how the wind moves the ribbons. This is now an Olympic event in the gymnastics category.

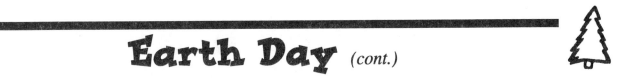

Have your students design posters for Earth Day. They can be displayed in the classroom, in the library, throughout the school, and in the community.

Hold an Earth Day bookmark contest. Have your class make up the contest rules and forms. Select a winner from each grade level. Duplicate the bookmarks of the winners and distribute them to the students at your school. See if your public library will duplicate and distribute them, too.

Set up an art center where students create art work from recyclable material including anything that they can use in a way different from the way it was originally used. This might include old buttons, fabric scraps, or lace trim as well as more typical "trash."

Make seed pictures. Draw simple shapes onto small pieces of colored tagboard. Glue a variety of seeds onto the shapes.

Create fruit and vegetable mobiles. Have students identify a grouping (e.g., vegetables that are seeds or fruits with pits) and draw, color, and cut out representative examples. Attach these to the bottoms of coat hangers with string or yarn. Mount the title from the top of the hanger.

Use the following quick-write topics or brainstorm some with your class: "If I were a seed. . ." "If I were a flower. . ." "I'd like to be a tree because . . ."

Learn about careers related to plants. Be sure to include nursery workers, landscape architects, gardeners, farmers, horticulturists, arborists, and botanists. Have students interview nursery workers or research the occupations and present their findings to the class. Invite some of these workers to school as guest speakers or take field trips to visit places of work.

Bibliography

Javana, John. *50 Simple Things Kids Can Do to Save the Earth.* Andrews and McMeel, 1990.

Lowery, Linda. *Earth Day.* Carolrhoda, 1992

Just A Dream

Author: Chris Van Allsburg

Publisher: Houghton Mifflin, 1990 (CAN: Thomas Allen & Son; UK, Gollancz Services; AUS, Jackaranda Wiley)

Summary: This book sends a powerful message about the importance of the environment. In a dream, a boy travels to a future world full of pollution and environmental problems.

Related Holidays: Earth Day is celebrated every year on April 22. Arbor Day is another holiday that relates to the earth because it is a time for planting trees.

Related Poetry: "Hug a Tree Today" by Susan M. Paprocki, *Special Day Celebrations* (Warren Publishing House, 1989), "Nature Is" by Jack Prelutsky, *The Random House Book of Poetry for Children* (Random House, 1983)

Related Songs: "It's Arbor Day Today" by Elizabeth McKinnon and "Trash Song" by Carol Mellott, *Special Day Celebrations* (Warren Publishing House, 1989).

Connecting Activities:

- Assess students' knowledge of environmental issues by completing a word web using the word "pollution" or "environment." Discuss the different types of pollution that exist in the world, especially any problems that are prevalent in your own community.

- Do a story map listing all the environmental events in the boy's dream. Have students write a sentence for each part of the story and illustrate it with crayon or marker. Tell where the boy went in each part of his dream. Ask the students if they noticed anything the same on each page. Remind them to look carefully, as the boy's cat follows him throughout the dream.

- Make a list of all the environmental mistakes that the boy saw during his dream. Discuss any unfamiliar vocabulary which relates to the book, such as wetlands and protected areas. Divide the class into small groups of four or five students. Assign each group one of the environmental mistakes. Have them discuss the mistake and come up with a list of possible solutions to the problem. Each group should make a detailed plan of action describing exactly what they would do.

- Discuss the informational book *50 Simple Things Kids Can Do To Save the Earth* by John Javna. See how many ideas your class can think of to save the earth. Compare your ideas to the ones found in the book. Put a star by any of the ideas which are already being implemented in your school or community.

- Each year the National Wildlife Federation produces a packet of classroom materials for use on Earth Day. The packet contains a teacher's guide, stamps, and an attractive poster showing the theme for Earth Day that year. Make a large banner that says "Earth Day Every Day." Decorate the banner with crayons or markers, drawing some of the many ways we can help our planet each day.

- An excellent resource book available for this holiday is called *Earth Day* by Linda Lowery. This book describes the history of Earth Day and gives many examples of ways in which people all over the world are working to improve our environment. The back of the book contains a list of environmental awareness ideas that children can follow at home, at play, and at school. A list of addresses for environmental organizations is also provided.

- Students can write letters to city officials, senators, representatives, and even the president, urging them to pass laws which protect the environment. Have them include some of their concerns and ideas for possible solutions.

- Create a bulletin board entitled "Our Dreams for Our Environment." Divide the board into halves labeled "good dreams" and "bad dreams." On the good side, put paintings or drawings which represent a clean, safe environment. On the bad side, put illustrations to represent what will happen to the environment if we don't take better care of the earth.

- Make a book to show some of the ways we can make every day an earth day. Color and cut out the cover provided on the following page for your Earth Day book.

- The first Arbor Day was celebrated in Nebraska on April, 10,1872. Although it is recognized on different days throughout the country, you may wish to celebrate it with Earth Day activities. Have someone from a forestry service or conservation group visit your class to talk about the importance of replanting trees. If possible, arrange with your parent teacher organization to purchase seedlings for each student to take home and plant. Gather together the student population and plant a tree on school property.

Earth Day Book Cover

See previous page for directions.

What Is a Plant?

A **plant** is a living thing. But, unlike an animal, a plant doesn't move around from one place to another to find food. A plant makes its own food right on the spot—right where it grows.

Color the plants on this page.

A Food-Chain Puzzle

Learn about the Food Chain. Cut out the puzzle pieces below. Glue the pieces together onto a sheet of construction paper. Color the pictures.

1. Decomposers turn waste into "food" for plants.

2. Green plants use food from the ground to grow.

3. Plant Eaters become food for meat eaters.

4. Meat Eaters make waste for the decomposers to use.

Endangered Animals

Nearly 800 different kinds of animals around the world are endangered. Endangered means that they are in danger of becoming extinct. When all the animals of a kind die and there are no more left to make babies, these animals are extinct.

Directions: Read the sentences below to find out how some endangered animals become extinct. Then color the animals.

Brown Bear

Some farmers shoot brown bears to keep them away from the farm animals.

Tiger

This big cat is killed for sport and for its fur. Its fur is used to make coats and rugs.

Orang-utan

People are cutting down the trees where orang-utans live to make space for new homes. The trees grow food for the orang-utans.

Garter Snake

The marshes where the San Francisco garter snakes live are being drained to build towns.

Bald Eagle

Factories wash poisons into the oceans. Fish and small animals swallow the poisons. Then, the bald eagle eats the poisoned fish and dies.

The Tropics

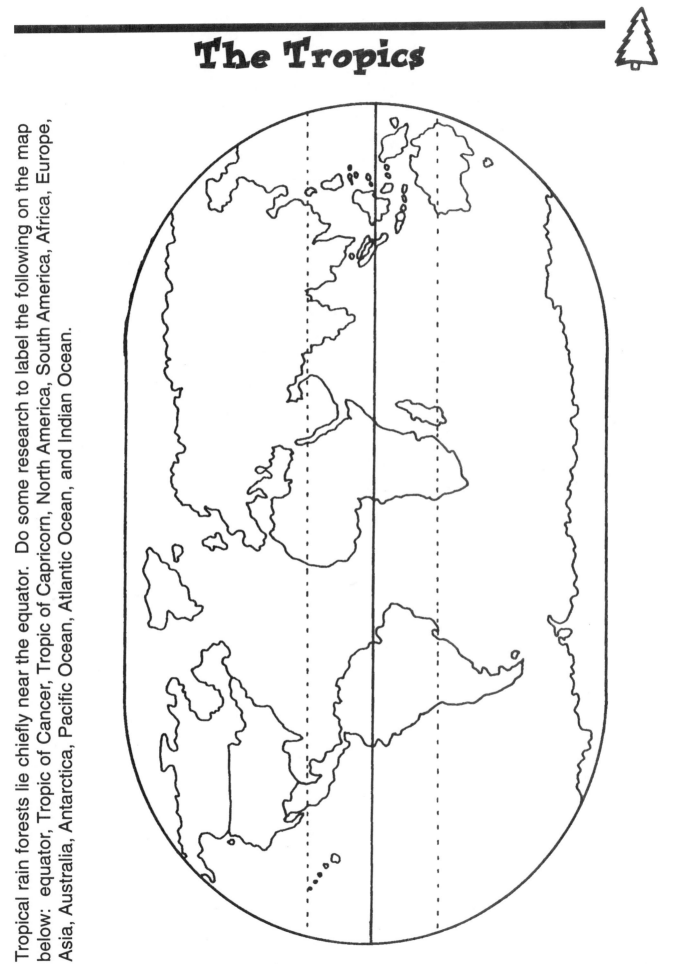

Tropical rain forests lie chiefly near the equator. Do some research to label the following on the map below: equator, Tropic of Cancer, Tropic of Capricorn, North America, South America, Africa, Europe, Asia, Australia, Antarctica, Pacific Ocean, Atlantic Ocean, and Indian Ocean.

Create Your Own Rain Forest

Since a rain forest may be inaccessible to you from your location, create a miniature version of the tropical region right in your classroom.

Materials:

a large fish tank, gravel, charcoal, compost, small stones, exotic plants (delicate ferns, small orchids, moss, bromeliads, etc.), water

Directions:

- Layer gravel and then charcoal (both available at an aquarium shop) on the bottom of the tank.
- Spread small stones over the gravel/charcoal layer; create small hills and valleys.
- Cover the stones with about an inch (2.54 cm) of compost.
- Dampen the compost with water and plant ferns, orchids, moss, and bromeliads. Allow plenty of growing space between plants.
- Cover the aquarium with a glass top. Keep in a warm spot out of direct sunlight.
- You may have to add a little water every few months.

Observe the rain forest at regular intervals. Record the date and time as well as any changes that have occurred. Measure any plant growth. Then, draw pictures or sketches to illustrate the findings.

Doorknob Hanging Tree

Materials:

- one pattern (on following page) for each child
- colored pencils or crayons
- scissors

Directions for the following page:

1. Read the message written on the tree.
2. Carefully cut out the small circle in the tree.
3. Then, color and cut out the large tree pattern.
4. Take your "Doorknob Hanging Tree" home and place it on the door you use the most!

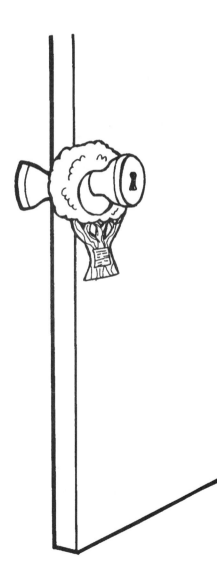

Doorknob Hanging Tree *(cont.)*

Cut out the circle

Thank you for remembering to conserve energy and to recycle. Every little bit helps to preserve wildlife!

Newspaper Tree

Materials:

- 4 double sheets of newspaper
- scissors
- extra newspaper
- coffee can or other container

Directions:

1. Spread out one sheet of newspaper and roll it up from the narrow end. Just before you reach the end, overlap another sheet to the end and continue rolling.

2. Continue the process until you have used all four pieces of newspaper.

3. Cut the top half of the roll into fours. (See picture below.)

4. Hold the roll at the bottom and carefully pull the "branches" out from the top of the tree.

5. "Plant" your tree in the container, using the extra paper to secure it. These trees can be used to create a rain forest scene, cornstalks for the fall holidays (Halloween and Thanksgiving), props for a play, or to add a tropical look to a reading area.

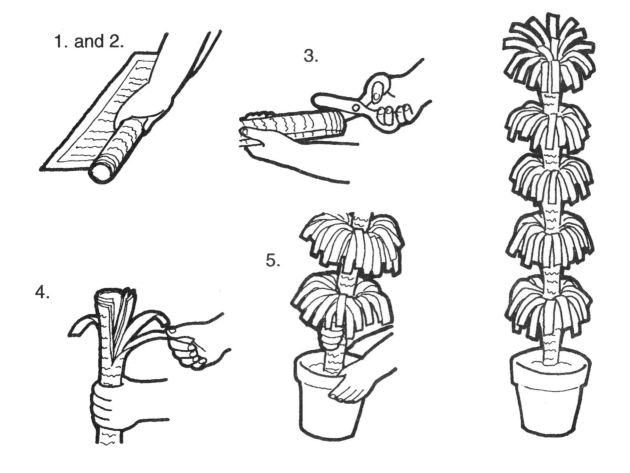

1. and 2.

3.

4.

5.

Tic-Tac-Earth

Materials: Make a copy of the two pages of Tic-Tac-Earth squares and an award certificate for each child.

Directions: Complete any three squares (projects) in a row (on either page) to win a "Save Our Earth Award."

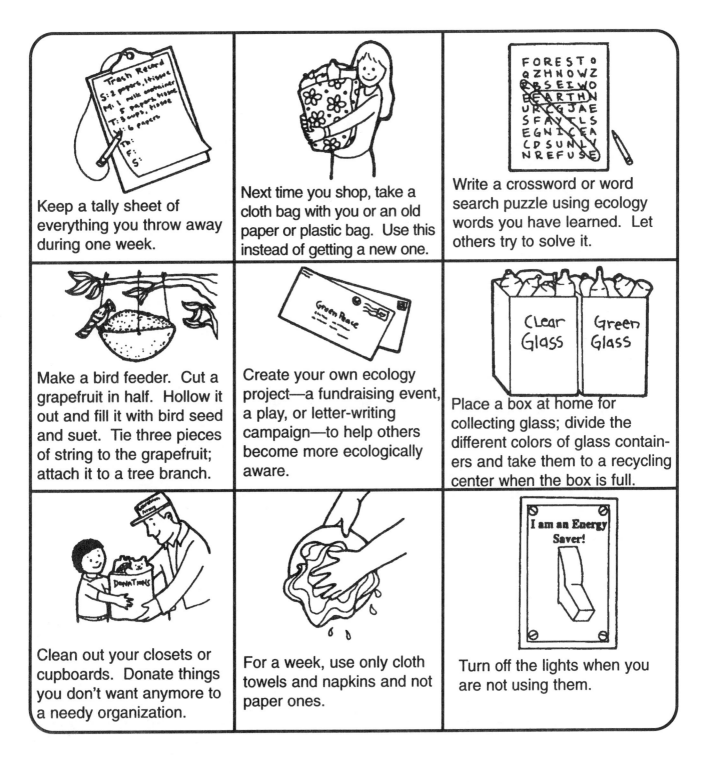

Keep a tally sheet of everything you throw away during one week.

Next time you shop, take a cloth bag with you or an old paper or plastic bag. Use this instead of getting a new one.

Write a crossword or word search puzzle using ecology words you have learned. Let others try to solve it.

Make a bird feeder. Cut a grapefruit in half. Hollow it out and fill it with bird seed and suet. Tie three pieces of string to the grapefruit; attach it to a tree branch.

Create your own ecology project—a fundraising event, a play, or letter-writing campaign—to help others become more ecologically aware.

Place a box at home for collecting glass; divide the different colors of glass containers and take them to a recycling center when the box is full.

Clean out your closets or cupboards. Donate things you don't want anymore to a needy organization.

For a week, use only cloth towels and napkins and not paper ones.

Turn off the lights when you are not using them.

Tic-Tac-Earth *(cont.)*

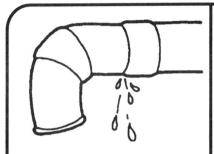 Find a water leak at home, at school, or in a local business. Report it.	 Snip each section of a six pack ring before you throw it out.	 Fill a 1 gallon plastic jug with water and some pebbles for weight. Place it in the toilet tank. This will save water every time the toilet is flushed!
 Next time you find a bug in your house or classroom, help it get back outside. Don't' kill it! Bugs have their places in our environment, too.	 Create an ecology newsletter to hand out to members of your community.	Begin using a recycling box at home for paper. Place all recyclable paper there rather than throwing it out.
 Construct art projects, puppets, posters, dioramas, or costumes out of recycled bags and boxes.	 Turn off the water while you brush your teeth. Turn it back on for rinsing.	Share something you've learned about ecology with your parents or other adults.

Save Our Earth
Award

_____
(Student name)

has demonstrated a love
of our earth by

_____

_____
Teacher signature

_____
Date